DELICIOUS AMERICAN BURGERS

ON THE GRILL

Donald Wallace

Table of Contents

BEEF BURGERS

Salsa Verde Burger

SERVINGS: 4

Ingredients

1. 2 tomatillos
2. 1 serrano chile pepper, sliced
3. 1/4 cup onion, sliced
4. 1/4 teaspoon chopped garlic
5. 1 teaspoon black pepper
6. 4 (93% lean) beef patties (4.75 ounces each)
7. 1/2 cup salsa verde
8. 4 slices reduced-fat pepper jack cheese
9. 4 whole-wheat hamburger buns
10. 1/4 cup shredded red cabbage
11. 4 ounces sliced avocado

Instructions

1. Place the tomatillos, Serrano peppers, onion, and garlic in a saucepan. Just cover with water and bring to a boil. Reduce heat to medium-low and cook until the tomatillos are soft and are slightly brown, about 20-30 minutes. Add more water if needed to keep from burning.

2. Pour cooked vegetables into a blender and blend until smooth.
3. Heat a skillet or grill over high heat.
4. When hot, spray with cooking spray or lightly oil. Add the patties.
5. Season with pepper and cook a few minutes on each side, as desired.
6. Add cheese and cover. Cook to melt, about 30 seconds.
7. Place the cooked burgers on the buns and top each with 2 tablespoons salsa verde, red cabbage, and avocado slices.

Sloppy Joe Burger

Ingredients

1. 1/3 cup of mayonnaise
2. 1/3 cup of sour cream
3. 1 tablespoon of apple cider vinegar
4. 1 ½ teaspoons of salt, divided
5. ¾ teaspoon of pepper, divided
6. 1 (16-ounce) package of tri-color coleslaw mix
7. 1 pound of ground sirloin
8. 2 tablespoons of steak sauce
9. 4 hamburger buns
10. 1 (16-ounce) can of chili, warmed

Instructions

1. Preheat grill on medium-high heat.
2. In a large bowl, whisk together mayonnaise, sour cream, apple cider vinegar, ½ teaspoon salt, and ¼ teaspoon pepper. Add coleslaw mix and toss to coat. Cover and chill until ready to serve.
3. Combine ground sirloin, steak sauce, and remaining 1 teaspoon of salt and ½ teaspoon of pepper. Shape into 4 equal patties.
4. Grill patties in a covered grill until desired doneness.
5. Serve on hamburger buns. Top with chili and coleslaw mix.

Swiss and Mushroom Burger

SERVINGS: 6

Ingredients

1. 1½ pounds of lean ground beef
2. ½ teaspoon of seasoned meat tenderizer
3. Salt and pepper, to taste
4. 2 teaspoons of butter
5. 2 (4-ounce) cans of sliced mushrooms, drained
6. 2 tablespoons of soy sauce
7. 4 slices of Swiss cheese
8. 6 hamburger buns

Instructions

1. Preheat grill on medium heat. Lightly oil grate.
2. Form ground beef into 6 patties. Season with meat tenderizer, salt, and pepper. Set aside.
3. In a skillet, melt butter over medium heat. Add mushrooms and soy sauce. Cook and stir until browned. Set aside and keep warm.
4. Grill for 6 minutes on each side or until desired doneness.
5. Divide mushroom mixture evenly among burgers and top each with a slice of Swiss cheese. Cover grill for 1 minute and allow cheese to melt.
6. Remove from grill and serve on hamburger buns.

Basil Burger

SERVINGS: **4**

Ingredients

1. 1¼ pounds of ground beef
2. 3 tablespoons of Worcestershire sauce
3. 1½ tablespoons of dried basil, or to taste
4. ¼ teaspoon of garlic salt
5. ¼ teaspoon of ground black pepper
6. 4 hamburger buns

Instructions

1. Preheat grill on high heat. Lightly oil the grill grate.
2. Mix ground beef, Worcestershire sauce, basil, garlic salt, and pepper in a bowl. Form into 4 equal patties.
3. Cook burgers for 6 minutes, turning once, until desired doneness.
4. Serve on hamburger buns.

Smokey Chili Burger

SERVINGS: **6**

Ingredients

1. 2 pounds of ground beef sirloin
2. ½ onion, grated
3. 1 tablespoon of grill seasoning
4. 1 tablespoon of liquid smoke
5. 2 tablespoons of Worcestershire sauce
6. 2 tablespoons of garlic, minced
7. 1 tablespoon of adobo sauce
8. 1 chipotle chili, chopped
9. Salt and pepper, to taste
10. 6 1-ounce slices of sharp cheddar cheese, optional
11. 6 hamburger buns

Instructions

1. Preheat grill on medium-high heat.
2. In a large bowl, combine ground sirloin, onion, grill seasoning, liquid smoke, Worcestershire sauce, garlic, adobo sauce, and chipotle pepper. Form into 6 equal patties, and season with salt and pepper.
3. Grill until burgers are no longer pink in the center. Place 1 slice of Cheddar cheese on each burger one minute before they are done.
4. Serve on hamburger buns.

Juicy Burger with Sun-Dried Tomatoes

SERVINGS: 8

Ingredients

1. 1 pound ground beef
2. 4 soft sun-dried tomatoes, chopped
3. 2 green onions, finely chopped
4. 2 cloves garlic, minced
5. ½ green bell pepper, chopped
6. 1 egg
7. 3 tablespoons bread crumbs
8. 1 dash Worcestershire sauce
9. 1 dash hot pepper sauce
10. salt and pepper, to taste
11. 1 teaspoon vegetable oil

Instructions

1. In a bowl, mix beef, sun-dried tomato, green onions, garlic, bell pepper, egg, bread crumbs, Worcestershire sauce, salt, and pepper together with your hands until well combined. Form into 8 patties.
2. In a skillet, heat vegetable oil over medium-high heat. Cook burgers in hot skillet for 5 to 6 minutes per side for well done, or until desired degree of doneness.

16

Skillet Burger

SERVINGS: **8**

Ingredients

1. 2 pounds of ground beef
2. 2 slices of bread, crustless, cubed
3. 2 tablespoons of milk
4. ¼ of an onion
5. 1 garlic clove
6. Spices of your choice
7. Oil
8. 8 hamburger buns
9. Condiments of your choice

Instructions

1. Mash bread and milk into a wet paste. Add onion, garlic, and spices.
2. Mix in the meat, and form into 8 equal patties.
3. Heat oil in the skillet and cook until desired doneness.
4. Serve on hamburger buns with desired condiments.

Cheddar Bacon Burger

SERVINGS: 4

Ingredients

1. 1 pound ground beef
2. 1/2 cup shredded Cheddar cheese
3. 2 tablespoons prepared horseradish
4. ½ teaspoon salt
5. ½ teaspoon pepper
6. ½ teaspoon garlic powder
7. ½ cup real bacon bits

Instructions

1. Preheat grill on high heat. Lightly oil the grill grate.
2. In a large bowl, mix together all ingredients with your hands. Shape into 4 patties.

3. Place hamburger patties on the grill, and cook for 5 minutes each side, or until well done.
4. Serve on buns.

Bayou Burger

SERVINGS: **4**

Ingredients

1. 1 pound of ground beef

2. ¼ cup of green onion, sliced

3. 1 teaspoon of seasoned salt

4. ¾ teaspoon of crushed dried basil

5. ½ teaspoon of garlic powder

6. ½ teaspoon of dried thyme

7. ½ teaspoon of hot pepper sauce

8. 4 hamburger buns

Instructions

1. Preheat grill to medium heat.
2. Mix ground beef, green onions, seasoned salt, basil, garlic powder, thyme, and hot pepper sauce in a large bowl. Shape into 4 equal patties. Grill until desired doneness, about 10 minutes.
3. Serve on hamburger buns.

Chili Cactus Burger

SERVINGS: 4

Ingredients

1. 1 ½ cups of water
2. 2 ancho chillies
3. 1 tablespoon of olive oil, divided
4. 2 garlic cloves
5. 1 teaspoon of sugar
6. ½ teaspoon of dried oregano
7. ½ teaspoon of ground cumin
8. ¼ teaspoon of freshly ground black pepper
9. 1 pound of lean ground sirloin
10. ⅜ teaspoon of kosher salt, divided
11. 2 medium cactus paddles
12. 1/3 cup of shredded peeled jicama
13. 3 tablespoons of cilantro leaves
14. 3 tablespoons of fresh lime juice
15. Cooking spray
16. 4 hamburger buns

Instructions

1. In a microwave-safe bowl combine 1½ cups water and chilies. Microwave on high for 2 minutes. Let stand for 15 minutes. Discard liquid, remove the stem and seed from the chilies.

2. Blend chilies, 1 teaspoon oil, and garlic in a food processor until smooth. In a medium bowl combine chili mixture, sugar, and next 4 ingredients (through beef). Stir in ¼ teaspoon of salt. Divide and shape into 4 equal patties.
3. Remove needles from cactus paddles with a knife. Peel and chop to measure 1 cup.
4. Heat a medium skillet over medium-high heat. Add remaining 2 teaspoons of oil. Add cactus paddles and sauté for 3 minutes, or until tender.
5. Preheat grill on medium-high heat.
6. In a small bowl combine cactus paddles, jicama, cilantro, and juice. Sprinkle with remaining ⅛ teaspoon salt.
7. Place patties on grill coated with cooking spray. Grill for 3 minutes. Turn patties and grill for 3 minutes longer or until desired doneness.
8. Serve on hamburger buns and top each with ¼ cup of jicama mix.

Sun-Dried Tomato and Blue Cheese Burgers

SERVINGS: 12

Ingredients

1. 3 pounds of ground beef
2. 1 cup of sun-dried tomatoes, diced
3. 4 ounces of blue cheese
4. ½ cup of chives, minced
5. 1 tablespoon of steak sauce
6. ¼ teaspoon of hot pepper sauce
7. ¼ tablespoon of Worcestershire sauce
8. 1 teaspoon of black pepper
9. 1 ½ teaspoons of salt
10. 1 teaspoon of dry mustard
11. 12 hamburger buns

Instructions

1. Mix ground beef, sun-dried tomatoes, blue cheese, chives, steak sauce, hot pepper sauce, Worcestershire sauce, black pepper, salt, and mustard in a large bowl. Cover and refrigerate for 2 hours.
2. Preheat grill on high heat.
3. Form mixture into 12 equal patties. Grill burgers for 5 minutes on each side or until desired doneness.
4. Serve on hamburger buns.

Whiskey & Beer Burger

SERVINGS: **6**

Ingredients

1. 1 ½ pounds ground beef
2. ¼ cup of favorite beer
3. 1 tablespoon Worcestershire sauce
4. 1 (1.5 fluid ounce) favorite whiskey
5. 2 teaspoons garlic powder
6. 1 teaspoon onion powder
7. 1 teaspoon salt
8. 1 teaspoon ground black pepper

Instructions

1. Preheat grill on medium-high heat. Lightly oil the grate.
2. Combine all ingredients in a bowl. Mix until evenly combined. Shape into 6 patties.
3. Cook on the preheated grill until the burgers are cooked to desired degree of doneness, or around 5 to 8 minutes each side.
4. Serve on buns.

Curry Garlic Burger

Ingredients

1. 2 pounds of lean ground beef
2. 1½ cups of chopped sweet onion
3. 1 egg, lightly beaten
4. 3 tablespoons of evaporated milk
5. 1 tablespoon of Worcestershire sauce
6. 3 large cloves of garlic, minced
7. 1 tablespoon of mild curry powder
8. 1 tablespoon of steak seasoning
9. 8 hamburger buns

Instructions

1. Preheat grill on high heat.
2. Mix beef, onion, egg, evaporated milk, Worcestershire sauce, garlic, curry powder, and steak seasoning in a bowl. Form into 8 patties.
3. Grill over indirect heat for 5 minutes on each side, or until desired doneness.
4. Serve on hamburger buns.

Bacon Wrapped Burger

SERVINGS: 4

Ingredients

1. 8 bacon slices
2. 1 (4.5-ounce) jar of sliced mushrooms, drained, chopped
3. ½ cup of sweet onion, chopped
4. 2 teaspoons of olive oil
5. ½ cup of honey barbecue sauce, divided
6. 1½ pounds of ground beef
7. Wooden picks
8. ¼ teaspoon of salt
9. 4 hamburger buns

Instructions

1. Preheat grill to medium-high heat.
2. Place bacon on a microwave-safe plate on top of paper towels. Cover with another paper towel and microwave on high for 2 minutes.
3. In a small non-stick skillet with oil, sauté mushrooms and onion over medium heat for 4 to 5 minutes, or liquid is absorbed and onions are tender. Remove from heat and stir in 2 tablespoons barbecue sauce.
4. Shape ground beef into 8 equal patties. Place 2 tablespoons of mushroom mix in the center of each of 4 patties. Top with remaining patties and press edges to seal. Wrap sides of each with 2 bacon

slices, making sure to overlap each slice. Secure bacon using wooden picks. Sprinkle patties with salt. Cover and chill for 10 minutes.

5. Grill patties with a covered lid for 5 to 6 minutes over medium-high heat. Flip and baste with half of remaining barbecue sauce. Grill for 5 to 6 minutes more. Turn again and baste with remaining barbecue sauce. Remove from grill, let stand for 5 minutes, and remove wooden picks.

6. Serve on hamburger buns, topped with remaining mushroom mixture.

Horseradish and Cheddar Cheese Burger

SERVINGS: 8

Ingredients

1. 2 pounds freshly minced beef brisket
2. 16 slices Cheddar cheese, cut into thinner than ¼-inch slices
3. 8 leaves romaine lettuce
4. Gherkin pickles, chopped
5. Freshly ground salt and black pepper
6. Ketchup
7. 8 buns

Grilled onions

1. 2 big onions, cut crossways into thinner than ¼-inch slices
2. Freshly ground salt and black pepper
3. 2 tablespoons olive oil

Horseradish mustard

1. 8 tablespoons Dijon mustard
2. 2 tablespoons drained horseradish

Instructions

1. Combine horseradish and mustard in a bowl and mix well.
2. Brush onions with olive oil and season with salt and pepper. Grill for approximately 4 minutes on each side.
3. Split beef into 8 burgers and sprinkle salt and pepper to taste. Grill for approximately 4 minutes on each side.
4. In the last minute of grilling, add 2 slices of cheese to every burger and let cheese melt.
5. Split each bun and place a burger in the middle. Top with horseradish mustard, grilled onions, lettuce, ketchup and gherkins before placing the other half of the bun on top.

Brisket Burger

SERVINGS: **6**

Ingredients

1. 2 pounds of beef brisket, ground
2. Kosher salt, to taste
3. Ground black pepper, to taste
4. 2 medium red onions, sliced
5. 1 medium yellow onion, sliced
6. 6 slices of cheddar cheese
7. 6 hamburger buns
8. 3 hearts of romaine, halved lengthwise
9. 3 whole dill pickles, sliced
10. 2 heirloom tomatoes, cored and sliced
11. Ketchup, mayonnaise, and mustard for serving

Instructions

1. Preheat grill on medium heat.
2. Shape ground brisket into 6 patties. Season with salt and pepper.
3. Heat a large cast-iron skillet on grill. Place patties in skillet and top with onion slices. Cover and cook 3 to 4 minutes and flip with onion slices on the bottom. Cook 2 more minutes. Top with cheese and cook 1 to 2 minutes longer, or until cheese is melted. Keep warm.
4. Grill buns, lettuce, pickles, and tomatoes in batches until charred, turning once
5. Serve burgers on hamburger buns with lettuce, pickles, and tomatoes as toppings.

Pizza Burger

SERVINGS: **12**

Ingredients

1. 2 pounds of ground beef
2. 24 slices of mozzarella cheese
3. 12 hamburger buns
4. 2 (6.5-ounce) cans of tomato sauce
5. 1 teaspoon of dried oregano
6. ½ teaspoon of dried minced onion
7. ½ teaspoon of salt
8. ¼ teaspoon of pepper
9. ¼ teaspoon of garlic powder

Instructions

1. Preheat grill on medium heat. Lightly oil the grate.
2. Shape ground beef into 12 patties.
3. Grill patties for 3 to 4 minutes on each side or until desired doneness. Place 2 slices of mozzarella cheese on each and place patties on hamburger buns.
4. In a bowl, mix tomato sauce, oregano, minced onion, salt, pepper, and garlic powder. Cover and heat in microwave for 5 minutes on High.
5. Spread tomato sauce mix over burgers and serve.

Spicy Salsa Burger

SERVINGS: 4

Ingredients

- 1 pound of ground beef
- 4 teaspoons of hot pepper sauce
- 4 tablespoons of salsa
- 4 slices of cheddar cheese
- 4 slices of Monterey Jack cheese
- 4 hamburger buns

Instructions

1. Preheat grill on high heat. Lightly oil the grate.
2. Form ground beef into 4 equal patties.
3. Grill patties over high heat for 2 to 4 minutes, and flip. Top cooked side of each patty with a dash of hot pepper sauce, a teaspoon of salsa, a slice of Cheddar cheese, and a slice of Monterey Jack cheese. Grill for 2 to 4 minutes more or to desired doneness.
4. Serve on hamburger buns.

Peanut Butter Bacon Burger

SERVINGS: 6

Ingredients

1. 1 pound of ground beef sirloin
2. 1 teaspoon of fresh ground black pepper
3. ½ teaspoon of onion powder
4. ½ teaspoon of garlic powder
5. ½ teaspoon of kosher salt
6. ½ teaspoon of Worcestershire sauce
7. ¼ teaspoon of cayenne pepper
8. 8 slices of Applewood-smoked bacon
9. 1 ½ cups of shredded sharp Cheddar cheese
10. 1 cup of peanut butter
11. 1 tablespoon of maple syrup
12. 6 hamburger buns
13. 6 leaves of lettuce
14. 2 tomatoes, sliced

Instructions

1. In a large bowl combine ground beef, black pepper, onion powder, garlic powder, salt, Worcestershire sauce, and cayenne pepper. Form into 6 equal patties. Transfer to a large plate and cover with plastic wrap. Refrigerate for half an hour.

2. Preheat grill on medium-high heat. Lightly oil the grate.
3. Place bacon in a large skillet over medium-high heat. Cook for about 10 minutes, occasionally turning, until browned. Drain on paper towels.
4. Grill patties for 4 minutes on each side or until desired doneness. Sprinkle Cheddar cheese over patties 1 minute before they are done.
5. In a microwave-safe bowl, mix peanut butter and maple syrup. Heat peanut butter mix in the microwave about 25 seconds, or until slightly runny. Stir again.
6. Spread peanut butter mix over hamburger buns and top with beef patties, lettuce, tomatoes, and bacon.

Bacon Bourbon Burger

SERVINGS: **2**

Ingredients

1. ½ pound of ground beef
2. 1 tablespoon of bourbon
3. 2 teaspoons of Worcestershire sauce
4. 2 teaspoons of brown sugar
5. 2 teaspoons of steak seasoning
6. ½ teaspoon of garlic salt
7. 2 slices of bacon, cooked
8. 2 slices of cheddar cheese
9. 2 hamburger buns
10. 2 tomato slices
11. 2 lettuce leaves

Instructions

1. Lightly oil the grate and preheat grill on high heat.
2. In a large bowl, mix ground beef, bourbon, Worcestershire sauce, brown sugar, steak seasoning, and garlic salt. Divide in half and shape into two equal patties.
3. Place on grill for 5 minutes. Flip over and top each with bacon and Cheddar cheese. Continue grilling until burgers are cooked to desired doneness.
4. Serve on buns and top with tomato slices and lettuce.

Cola Burger

Ingredients

1. 1 egg
2. ½ cup of cola-flavored carbonated beverage, divided
3. ½ cup of crushed saltine crackers
4. 6 tablespoons of French salad dressing, divided
5. 2 tablespoons of grated parmesan cheese
6. 1½ pounds of ground beef
7. 6 hamburger buns

Instructions

1. Lightly oil the grate. Preheat grill on high heat.
2. Mix together egg, ¼ cup of cola, crackers, 2 tablespoons of French dressing, and grated parmesan cheese in a medium bowl. Add the ground beef and mix well. Form into 6 patties. Pour remaining cola and dressing in a bowl. Mix well.
3. Grill burgers 3 minutes on each side. Brush with dressing and cola. Grill for 8 to 10 more minutes, occasionally basting.
4. Serve on hamburger buns.

Sweet Garlic BBQ Burger

Ingredients

1. 2 pounds of ground beef
2. 1 pound of ground pork
3. 2 (1-ounce) packages of dry onion soup mix
4. ¾ cup of barbecue sauce
5. ½ cup of an onion, chopped
6. Garlic salt, to taste
7. 9 hamburger buns

Instructions

1. Preheat grill on medium-high heat. Lightly oil the grate.
2. In a large bowl, combine ground beef, ground pork, onion soup mix, barbecue sauce, chopped onion, and garlic salt. Form into 9 patties.
3. Grill until desired doneness and serve on hamburger buns.

Crunchy Onion Burger

SERVINGS: **6**

Ingredients

1. 2 pounds extra lean ground beef
2. 1 (1-ounce) package of dry onion soup mix
3. 1 egg, beaten
4. 2 teaspoons of hot pepper sauce
5. 2 teaspoons of Worcestershire sauce
6. ¼ teaspoon of ground black pepper
7. ¾ cup of rolled oats
8. 6 hamburger buns

Instructions

1. Preheat grill on medium-high heat and lightly oil the grate.
2. Combine beef, onion soup mix, egg, hot sauce, and oats in a large bowl. Shape into 6 equal patties.
3. Grill patties for 10 to 20 minutes, or to desired doneness.
4. Serve on hamburger buns.

Barbecue Citrus Burger

SERVINGS: 4

Ingredients

1. 1 lemon
2. 1 lime
3. 1 orange
4. 1 tablespoon of barbecue sauce
5. 1 pound of ground beef
6. ¼ cup of barbecue sauce
7. 4 slices of pepper jack cheese
8. 4 hamburger buns

Instructions

1. In a large bowl, grate the zest from the lemon, lime, and orange. Squeeze juice from half of each piece of fruit into the bowl. Whisk in 1 tablespoon barbecue sauce, stir in ground beef, and mix well. Cover and refrigerate for 10 to 30 minutes.
2. Lightly oil the grate and preheat grill on high heat.
3. Form into 4 patties and grill with open lid for 3 minutes on each side. Brush each burger with one tablespoon barbecue sauce during grilling, making sure to coat both sides. Top with pepper jack cheese and cook for 1 more minute.
4. Serve on buns.

Horseradish Muenster Burger

SERVINGS: 4

Ingredients

- 1½ pounds of ground beef
- ½ cup of steak sauce, divided
- 2 tablespoons of horseradish
- 2 tablespoons of fresh parsley, finely chopped
- 2 tablespoons of green onion, finely chopped
- 4 slices of Muenster cheese
- 4 hamburger buns

Instructions

1. Heat grill on high heat.
2. Combine 6 tablespoons of steak sauce, horseradish, parsley, and green onion in a bowl. Form ground beef into 4 equal patties.
3. Place patties on the grill and brush with remaining steak sauce. Grill for 6 to 8 minutes on each side, or until desired doneness.
4. Top with Muenster cheese and horseradish sauce.
5. Serve on hamburger buns.

Italian Burger

Ingredients

1. 3 pounds of lean ground beef
2. 1 pound of Italian sausage
3. 1 tablespoon of onion, minced
4. 1 teaspoon of garlic, minced
5. 2 teaspoons of Italian seasoning
6. 1 tablespoon of light olive oil
7. 1 teaspoon of salt
8. 1 teaspoon of ground black pepper
9. 2 teaspoons of anise seed
10. ¼ cup of melted butter
11. 6 baguettes, split

Instructions

1. Mix ground beef, sausage, onion, garlic, Italian seasoning, olive oil, salt, pepper, and anise seed in a bowl. Refrigerate for 1 hour, then mix again afterwards.

2. Divide mixture into 12 portions and form into long burgers with rounded edges approximately 4 inches wide and 12 inches long.
3. Lightly oil the grate. Preheat grill on medium heat.
4. Preheat oven to 250°F (120°C). Lightly brush butter on the cut sides of baguettes.
5. Grill for 7 to 8 minutes on each side, or until done. 5 minutes before burgers are done, lay baguette halves on grill. Toast until each side is browned.
6. Place each burger into a baguette, close it, and wrap with aluminum foil.
7. Bake sandwiches in preheated oven for 15 minutes.

Serve.

Juicy Garlic Burger

Ingredients

1. 2 pounds of ground beef
2. 1 egg, beaten
3. ¾ cup of dry bread crumbs
4. 3 tablespoons of evaporated milk
5. 2 tablespoons of Worcestershire sauce
6. ⅛ teaspoon of cayenne pepper
7. 2 cloves of garlic, minced
8. 8 hamburger buns

Instructions

1. Lightly oil the grill grate. Preheat grill on high heat.
2. Mix ground beef, egg, bread crumbs, evaporated milk, Worcestershire sauce, cayenne pepper, and garlic in a large bowl. Form into 8 equal patties.
3. Grill patties 5 minutes on each side or until desired doneness.
4. Serve on hamburger buns.

Teriyaki Onion Burger

SERVINGS: **4**

Ingredients

1. 1 pound of ground beef
2. ¼ cup of teriyaki marinade sauce
3. 1 (3-ounce) can of French-fried onions
4. 4 slices of cheddar cheese
5. 4 hamburger buns

Instructions

1. Preheat grill on high heat.
2. In a bowl, mix together ground beef, teriyaki marinade and French-fried onions. Form into 4 equal patties.
3. Lightly oil the grill grate. Grill patties until desired doneness.
4. Top with cheese and serve on hamburger buns.

CHICKEN

BURGERS

Chicken Tartar Burger

SERVINGS: 8

Ingredients

1. ½ cup of green bell pepper, chopped
2. ½ cup of red bell pepper, chopped
3. ¼ cup of fresh cilantro, chopped
4. 1 small onion, chopped
5. 2 cloves of garlic, minced
6. 1 teaspoon of hot sauce
7. Salt, to taste
8. Pepper, to taste
9. 2 pounds of ground chicken
10. 1 cup of dry bread crumbs
11. 8 hamburger buns
12. 8 iceberg lettuce leaves

For Sauce:
1. 3 tablespoons of mayonnaise
2. 1 tablespoon of dill pickle relish
3. 1 tablespoon of hot sauce
4. 1 clove of garlic, minced
5. 1 tablespoon of lime juice

Instructions

1. For the tart sauce: Stir together mayonnaise, relish, hot sauce, garlic, and lime juice in a small bowl. Cover and refrigerate for half an hour.
2. For the chicken burgers: Combine together green pepper, red pepper, cilantro, onion, garlic, hot sauce, salt, and pepper in a large bowl. Mix chicken with hand until well combined. Sprinkle on bread

crumbs and continue mixing. Divide and form into 8 patties.
3. Preheat grill on medium-high heat. Lightly oil the grate.
4. Grill patties until desired doneness.
5. Spread cut sides of hamburger buns with tartar sauce. Add a chicken patty and top with lettuce to serve.

Orange Chicken Burger

SERVINGS: 4

Ingredients

1. 1 pound of ground chicken
2. ½ (1-ounce) package of guacamole seasoning mix
3. ½ cup of fresh cilantro, chopped, divided
4. ½ lime, juiced
5. ¼ cup of onion, minced
6. 4 hamburger buns
7. ¼ cup of salsa, divided
8. 4 slices of cheddar cheese

Instructions

1. Preheat grill on medium heat. Lightly oil the grate.
2. Mix together ground chicken, guacamole seasoning, half of the cilantro, lime juice, and minced onion in a bowl until combined. Form into 4 patties. Reserve the other half of cilantro for garnish.
3. Grill chicken burgers until desired doneness.
4. Two minutes before burgers are done, place buns onto grill to toast, about 1 minute on each side. Top each with a slice of cheddar cheese and let it melt.
5. Serve chicken burgers on toasted hamburger buns. Top with 1 tablespoon of salsa and 1 tablespoon of reserved chopped cilantro.

Green Chili Guacamole Chicken Burger

SERVINGS: 4

Ingredients

1. 1 pound of ground chicken breast
2. 1 4-ounce can of chopped green chili peppers, drained
3. 1 fresh jalapeño pepper, seeded, diced
4. 3 green onions, chopped
5. 1 tablespoon of dried oregano
6. 1 teaspoon of salt
7. 1 teaspoon of garlic powder
8. Black pepper, to taste
9. 4 slices of cheddar cheese
10. 4 hamburger buns
11. 1 cup of shredded lettuce
12. 1/3 cup of salsa

For Sauce:

1. 1 avocado, peeled, pitted
2. ½ cup of fresh cilantro leaves
3. 2 tablespoons of sour cream
4. ½ teaspoon of chili powder
5. Salt, to taste
6. Pepper, to taste

Instructions

1. For the guacamole: Blend avocado, cilantro, sour cream, chili powder, salt, and pepper in a food processor and pulse until smooth.
2. Combine chicken, canned chilies, jalapeño pepper, green onions, oregano, salt, garlic powder, and pepper in a bowl. Form into 4 patties.
3. Preheat grill on medium heat. Lightly oil the grate.
4. Grill each patty for 5 minutes on each side, or until well done. Keep warm and top each with a slice of cheddar cheese. Lightly grill buns while cheese is melting.
5. Spread bottom of each bun with guacamole and top with ¼ cup of shredded lettuce and a grilled chicken burger. Spoon 1 tablespoon of salsa on each burger and top with the other half of the bun to serve.

Thai Chicken Burger

SERVINGS: 8

Ingredients

1. 1 cup of mayonnaise
2. ¼ cup of flaked coconut, chopped
3. 1 tablespoon of fresh mint, chopped
4. 2 pounds of ground chicken
5. 2½ cups of panko bread crumbs
6. ½ cup of Thai peanut sauce
7. 2 tablespoons of red curry paste
8. 2 tablespoons of green onion, minced
9. 2 tablespoons of fresh parsley, minced
10. 2 teaspoons of soy sauce
11. 3 cloves of garlic, minced
12. 2 teaspoons of lemon juice
13. 2 teaspoons of lime juice
14. 1 tablespoon of hot pepper sauce
15. 8 hamburger buns

Instructions

1. Preheat grill on medium heat.
2. Mix mayonnaise, coconut, and mint in a small bowl. Cover and refrigerate for 1 hour.
3. Combine ground chicken, panko crumbs, Thai peanut sauce, curry paste, green onion, parsley, soy sauce, garlic, lemon juice, lime juice, and hot pepper sauce in a large bowl. Divide and form into 8 patties.
4. Grill until desired doneness.
5. Serve on toasted buns with coconut mint mayonnaise mixture.

Grilled Chicken Burgers with Slaw

SERVINGS: 4

Ingredients

1. 1 tablespoon butter
2. 1 small red onion, one half sliced in rings and one half diced
3. 2 cloves garlic, chopped
4. 2 tablespoons tomato paste
5. 1 teaspoon sugar
6. 1 tablespoon Worcestershire sauce
7. 1 tablespoon hot sauce
8. 1 ¼ pounds ground chicken
9. 1 tablespoon grill seasoning
10. 3 tablespoons extra virgin olive oil
11. 2 tablespoons honey
12. 1 lemon juice
13. 3 tablespoons sweet pickle relish
14. 2 cups shredded cabbage combination
15. Salt and pepper
16. 4 Kaiser rolls

Instructions

1. Use a skillet and melt butter over medium heat. Add the chopped onions, garlic, and tomato paste, and simmer for 5 minutes. Gradually add the sugar and transfer it to a bowl. Let cool for 5 minutes. Add Worcestershire and hot sauce. Mix well.
2. Place chicken into bowl and combine, evenly distributing all the flavors. Form 4 patties.
3. Preheat grill on medium-high heat. Grill for 5 minutes on each side.
4. Mix olive oil, honey, and lemon juice in a dish. Add relish, sliced onions, and cabbage mix. Season with salt and pepper. Mix to coat.
5. Top bun bottoms with slaw, burgers, and place bun tops over the burgers.

Avocado Chicken Burger

SERVINGS: 4

Ingredients

1. 1 ripe avocado, sliced
2. 1 tablespoon of lemon juice
3. 1 tablespoon of butter
4. 1 large onion, sliced
5. 4 chicken breast halves, boneless, skinless
6. Salt, to taste
7. Pepper, to taste
8. 4 hamburger buns
9. 4 tablespoons mayonnaise
10. 4 slices provolone cheese

Instructions

1. Preheat grill on high heat. Lightly oil the grate.
2. Combine sliced avocado and lemon juice in a small bowl. Add water to cover and set aside.
3. In a large skillet heat butter over medium-high heat. Sauté onions until browned and caramelized, and set aside.
4. Season chicken with salt and pepper, to taste. Grill until no longer pink and juices run clear, about 5 minutes on each side. Place buns on grill to toast.
5. Spread buns with mayonnaise, and layer with chicken, caramelized onion, provolone and avocado to serve.

FISH BURGERS

Rosemary Salmon Burger

SERVINGS: **8**

Ingredients

1. 2 ½ pounds of salmon fillets, skinned, de-boned
2. 1 cup of dry bread crumbs
3. ½ cup of red onion, minced
4. 1 tablespoon of Dijon mustard
5. 2 teaspoons of horseradish
6. 2 eggs, beaten
7. 1 tablespoon of fresh rosemary, minced
8. ½ teaspoon of salt
9. ½ teaspoon of black pepper
10. 2 tablespoons of olive oil
11. 8 hamburger buns

Instructions

1. Remove bones from salmon and mince.
2. Mix the minced salmon with bread crumbs, red onion, Dijon mustard, horseradish, and eggs in a large bowl. Season with rosemary, salt, and pepper.
3. Chill for half hour in refrigerator.
4. Preheat grill on medium-high heat. Lightly oil the grate.
5. Form salmon mix into 8 equal patties.
6. Grill until desired doneness, then serve on hamburger buns.

Lemon Garlic Tuna Burger

SERVINGS: 4

Ingredients

1. 2 (6-ounce) cans of tuna, drained, flaked
2. ½ cup of panko bread crumbs
3. ¼ cup of green onions, chopped
4. 3 tablespoons of fresh parsley, minced
5. 2 cloves of garlic, minced
6. ¼ teaspoon each of salt and pepper
7. Juice of half a lemon
8. 3 tablespoons of sour cream
9. 1 egg
10. 4 English muffins
11. 4 leaves of lettuce
12. 1 tomato, sliced

Instructions

1. Mix tuna, bread crumbs, green onion, parsley, garlic, salt, pepper, lemon, sour cream, and egg, in a bowl by hand. Form into 4 patties. Bake for 20 minutes on a greased baking sheet at 400°F (200°C).

2. Serve on toasted English muffins with lettuce and tomato. Spread sour cream on each burger if desired, and serve.

Bacon Salmon Burger

SERVINGS: **2**

Ingredients

1. 1 ½ pounds of salmon, boneless, skinless, chopped
2. 4 slices of onion
3. 4 slices of tomato
4. 8 slices of cucumber
5. 4 slices of cooked bacon
6. 2 teaspoons of parsley
7. 2 teaspoons of chives
8. 2 hamburger buns, buttered
9. Salt
10. Pepper
11. Canola oil
12. Mustard

Instructions

1. Combine salmon, chives, parsley, salt, and pepper. Form into 2 patties.
2. Add canola oil to the pan and heat. Cook in oil for 15 minutes on each side.
3. Remove from the pan and place on buttered buns.
4. Add onion, tomatoes, bacon, cucumber, and mustard.
5. Serve on buns.

Red pepper Mayonnaise Tuna Burger

SERVINGS: 4

Ingredients

1. 1 (6-ounce) can of tuna, drained
2. 1 egg
3. ½ cup of Italian bread crumbs
4. 1/3 cup of onion, minced
5. ¼ cup of celery, minced
6. ¼ cup of red bell pepper, minced
7. ¼ cup of mayonnaise
8. 2 tablespoons of chili sauce
9. ½ teaspoon of dried dill weed
10. ¼ teaspoon of salt
11. ⅛ teaspoon of black pepper
12. 1 dash of hot pepper sauce
13. 1 dash of Worcestershire sauce
14. 4 hamburger buns
15. 1 tomato, sliced
16. 4 leaves of lettuce

Instructions

1. Combine tuna, egg, bread crumbs, onion, celery, red bell pepper, mayonnaise, hot chili sauce, chili sauce, dill, salt, pepper, hot pepper sauce and Worcestershire sauce. Form into 4 patties and refrigerate for 40 minutes.
2. Spray a skillet with cooking spray. Fry patties until desired doneness. Turning carefully.
3. Serve on buns with tomato slices and lettuce.

Lemon Salmon Burger

SERVINGS: **6**

Ingredients

1. 1 (16-ounce) can of salmon, drained, flaked
2. 2 eggs
3. ¼ cup of fresh parsley, chopped
4. 2 tablespoons of onion, chopped
5. ¼ cup of Italian dry bread crumbs
6. 2 tablespoons of lemon juice
7. ½ teaspoon of dried basil
8. 1 pinch of red pepper flakes
9. 1 tablespoon of vegetable oil

For Dressing:

1. 2 tablespoons of mayonnaise
2. 1 tablespoon of lemon juice
3. 1 pinch of dried basil

Instructions

1. In a medium bowl, combine salmon, eggs, parsley, onion, breadcrumbs, 2 tablespoons of lemon juice, dried basil, and red pepper. Form into 6 patties.
2. Heat oil in a large skillet over medium heat. Add patties to skillet and cook until browned.
3. Mix mayonnaise, 1 tablespoon of lemon juice, and basil in a small bowl.
4. Serve patties with mayonnaise mix on a bun.

Tilapia Burger

Ingredients

1. 1½ pounds of tilapia fillets, frozen, skinless
2. ⅔ cups of breadcrumbs
3. 1 egg, plus 1 egg white, beaten
4. 2 tablespoons of spicy brown mustard
5. 2 teaspoons of garlic, minced
6. 1 teaspoon of salt
7. ½ teaspoon of black pepper
8. ½ teaspoon of dried oregano
9. 1 teaspoon of smoked paprika
10. 2 medium jalapeños, seeded, chopped
11. 1 small red onion, diced
12. Olive oil
13. 6 hamburger buns
14. ½ cup of salsa
15. ½ cup of sour cream

Instructions

1. Cut tilapia into cubes and blend in a food processor.
2. Add eggs, breadcrumbs, garlic, mustard, salt, pepper, smoked paprika, and oregano. Mix well, and stir in onion and jalapeño.

3. Lightly oil a large skillet and heat over medium heat.
4. Divide and form into 6 patties.
5. Cook until golden on each side.
6. Transfer to a plate and cover with foil.
7. Repeat with remaining burgers.
8. Toast buns and serve burgers topped with salsa and sour cream.

OTHER MEAT

BURGERS

Great Plains Bison Burger

SERVINGS: 4

Ingredients

1. 1 ear of corn, shucked
2. 1 small red onion, sliced
3. Cooking spray
4. 2 tablespoons of mayonnaise
5. 1 teaspoon of mustard seeds
6. 1 teaspoon of apple cider vinegar
7. ⅜ teaspoon of salt, divided
8. 1 tablespoon of adobo sauce
9. 1 ½ ounces of corn chips
10. 1 tablespoon of fresh sage, chopped
11. ½ teaspoon of garlic powder
12. ½ teaspoon of black pepper
13. 1 pound of ground bison
14. 4 hamburger buns

Instructions

1. Preheat grill on high heat. Lightly oil the grate.

2. Place corn and onion on grill rack. Cook until charred, occasionally turning corn and turning onion once.
3. Cut kernels from ears of corn. Combine corn, mayonnaise, mustard seeds, vinegar, and ⅛ teaspoon of salt. Process in a blender until smooth.
4. Combine onion and adobo sauce.
5. Place chips in a food processor and pulse 15 times, or until coarsely chopped. Combine chips, ¼ teaspoon salt, sage, garlic powder, pepper, and bison. Mix well. Divide and Form into 4 equal patties.
6. Grill patties for 3 minutes, turn, and continue grilling until desired doneness.
7. Place 1 patty on bottom half of each hamburger bun. Spread 1 tablespoon of corn mix over each patty, and top with onion mixture. Top with hamburger top.

Garlic Mayo and Onion Bison Burger

SERVINGS: 4

Ingredients

1. 1 pound of ground bison
2. 1 pound of ground beef sirloin
3. 1 yellow onion, minced
4. 4 cloves of garlic, minced
5. 2 tablespoons of chopped fresh parsley
6. 1 tablespoon of onion powder
7. 1 tablespoon of garlic powder
8. 1 teaspoon of seasoning salt
9. ¼ cup of ketchup
10. 2 tablespoons of Worcestershire sauce
11. Black pepper, to taste
12. Salt, optional
13. Olive oil
14. 4 hamburger buns

For Onions:
1. 2 tablespoons of bacon fat
2. 1 yellow onion, sliced

3. Salt, to taste
4. Black pepper, to taste

For Sauce:
1. ½ cup of prepared mayonnaise
2. 2 tablespoons of chopped fresh parsley
3. 4 cloves of raw garlic, chopped
4. Salt, to taste
5. Black pepper, to taste

Instructions

1. In a large bowl mix bison, beef sirloin, onions, garlic, and parsley. Add onion powder, garlic powder, seasoning salt, ketchup, Worcestershire, and a few turns of freshly ground black pepper. Mix well.
2. Cook a small portion of meat mix in a large sauté pan over medium-high heat. Add salt to taste. Divide and form into 4 equal patties. Set aside.
3. In a large sauté pan, heat bacon fat over medium-high heat and add onions. Cook for 1 minute and then season with salt, to taste. Cook onions about 8 to 10 minutes, until caramelized, stirring frequently. Remove from heat and set aside.
4. In a bowl, combine mayonnaise, parsley, garlic, salt, and pepper. Mixing well.
5. Assemble burgers with onions and sauce, serving on hamburger buns.

Spicy Lamb Burger

Ingredients

1. 1 pound of ground lamb
2. 2 tablespoons of fresh mint leaves, chopped
3. 2 tablespoons of fresh cilantro, chopped
4. 2 tablespoons of fresh oregano, chopped
5. 1 tablespoon of garlic, chopped
6. 1 teaspoon of sherry
7. 1 teaspoon of white wine vinegar
8. 1 teaspoon of molasses
9. 1 teaspoon of ground cumin
10. ¼ teaspoon of ground allspice
11. ½ teaspoon of red pepper flakes
12. ½ teaspoon of salt
13. ½ teaspoon of black pepper
14. 4 pita bread rounds
15. 4 ounces of feta cheese, crumbled

Instructions

1. Preheat grill on medium heat.
2. In a large bowl, mix the lamb with mint, cilantro, oregano, garlic, sherry, vinegar, and molasses. Season with cumin, allspice, red pepper flakes, salt, and black pepper, and combine. Shape into 4 equal patties.
3. Lightly oil the grate. Grill burgers until well done.

4. Heat pita pocket quickly on grill.
5. Serve burgers wrapped in pitas with feta cheese.

Cilantro Lamb Burger

SERVINGS: **5**

Ingredients

1. 1¼ pounds of ground lamb
2. 1 egg
3. 1 teaspoon of dried oregano
4. 1 teaspoon of dry sherry
5. 1 teaspoon of white wine vinegar
6. ½ teaspoon of crushed red pepper flakes
7. 4 cloves of garlic, minced
8. ½ cup of green onions, chopped
9. 1 tablespoon of chopped fresh mint
10. 2 tablespoons of chopped fresh cilantro
11. 2 tablespoons of dry bread crumbs
12. ⅛ teaspoon of salt
13. ¼ teaspoon of black pepper
14. 5 hamburger buns

Instructions

1. Preheat grill on medium-high heat. Lightly oil the grate.
2. Combine and mix the lamb, egg, oregano, sherry, vinegar, red pepper flakes, garlic, green onions,

mint, cilantro, bread crumbs, salt, and pepper together by hand. Form into 5 equal patties.
3. Grill until desired doneness and serve on buns.

Pork Apple Burger

SERVINGS: 8

Ingredients

1. 2 pounds of ground pork
2. 1 apple, peeled, cored, chopped
3. 1 sweet onion, chopped
4. 3 cloves of garlic, minced
5. ¼ cup of teriyaki sauce
6. 1 egg
7. 8 hamburger buns
8. 1 (20-ounce) can of sliced pineapples, drained

Instructions

1. Preheat grill on medium-high heat.
2. Mix together ground pork, apple, onion, garlic, teriyaki sauce, and egg in a large bowl. Add some juice from the can of pineapple if too dry. Form into 8 patties.
3. Lightly oil grate and grill pork burgers until desired doneness.
4. Toast buns on grill.
5. Serve burgers on toasted buns, topped with pineapple slices.

Garlic Egg Turkey Burger

SERVINGS: 4

Ingredients

1. 1 pound of ground turkey
2. 1 tablespoon of garlic powder
3. 1 tablespoon of red pepper flakes
4. 1 teaspoon of dried minced onion, optional
5. 1 egg
6. ½ cup of cheese crackers, crushed
7. 4 hamburger buns

Instructions

1. Preheat grill on high heat.
2. Combine ground turkey, garlic powder, red pepper flakes, minced onion, egg and crackers in a large bowl by hand. Form into 4 equal patties.
3. Grill until desired doneness, about 5 minutes on each side.
4. Serve on hamburger buns.

Cheddar Onion Turkey Burger

SERVINGS: **6**

Ingredients

1. ¾ cup of sweet onion, chopped
2. 1/3 cup of wheat germ
3. 1½ teaspoons of ancho chili powder
4. ¾ teaspoon of ground cumin
5. ½ teaspoon of salt
6. ¼ teaspoon of ground red pepper
7. 1 ½ pounds of ground turkey breast
8. Cooking spray
9. 4 ounces of extra sharp cheddar cheese, sliced
10. 6 slices of sweet onion
11. 6 hamburger buns
12. 6 tablespoons of spicy ketchup

Instructions

1. Preheat grill for medium heat. Lightly oil the grate.
2. Combine first 7 ingredients in a large bowl, and divide into 6 equal patties.
3. Grill until nearly done. Divide cheese over patties, and continue grilling until desired doneness. Remove from grill and let cool for 5 minutes.
4. Place onion slices on grill rack coated with cooking spray. Grill until browned and tender.
5. Serve on hamburger buns, placing 1 patty on bottom half of each bun and top with an onion slice, spicy ketchup, and top half of bun.

VEGGIE BURGERS

Korean BBQ Veggie Burger

SERVINGS: **8**

Ingredients

1. 1 (15.5 ounce) can garbanzo beans, drained and mashed
2. 8 fresh basil leaves, chopped
3. ¼ cup oat bran
4. ¼ cup quick cooking oats
5. 1 cup cooked brown rice
6. 1 (14 ounce) package firm tofu
7. 5 tablespoons Korean barbeque sauce
8. ½ teaspoon salt
9. ½ teaspoon ground black pepper
10. ¾ teaspoon garlic powder
11. ¾ teaspoon dried sage
12. 2 teaspoons vegetable oil

Instructions

1. Stir together mashed garbanzo beans and basil in a large bowl. Mix in oat bran, quick oats, and rice.
2. In a different bowl, mash tofu with your hands, squeezing as much water as possible. Drain and repeat until there is barely any water left.
3. Pour barbeque sauce over the tofu, and completely coat. Stir in the tofu with the garbanzo beans and

oats. Season with salt, pepper, garlic powder, and sage. Mix until well blended.
4. Heat oil over medium-high heat in a large skillet.
5. Form patties out of the bean mix, and fry in hot oil for about 5 minutes on each side.
6. Serve on burger buns.

Garbanzo Bean Patties

SERVINGS: **12**

Ingredients

1. 1 (16 ounce) package dry garbanzo beans (chickpeas)
2. 1 onion, chopped
3. 1 tablespoon dried thyme
4. salt and pepper to taste
5. 2 ½ cups dry bread cubes
6. 2 eggs, beaten
7. 4 tablespoons vegetable oil

Instructions

1. Place garbanzo beans with 12 cups water in a large pot. Cook over medium heat for 2 1/2 to 3 hours, or until tender. Check occasionally, and add more water if needed.
2. In a blender blend small batches of the garbanzo beans on chop or blend setting, until mix is a paste. Add onions, thyme, salt and pepper to the mixture, mixing well.
3. Add bread cubes and egg, and mix well. Form mixture into patties.
4. Heat oil in a large skillet over medium heat. Fry patties until each side is golden brown.

Tofu and Plantain Patties

SERVINGS: **5**

Ingredients

1. 1 ¼ cups cubed tofu
2. 1 ¼ cups chopped zucchini
3. 1 plantain, peeled and sliced
4. ½ cup canned sliced mushrooms
5. ½ cup sun-dried tomatoes
6. ½ cup bread crumbs
7. ¼ cup black olives
8. 1 large clove garlic, roughly chopped
9. 1 tablespoon butter, or as needed

Instructions

1. In a blender or food processor, blend tofu, zucchini, plantain, mushrooms, sun-dried tomatoes, bread crumbs, olives, and garlic until well mixed and thick. Form into 5 patties.
2. Heat butter over medium heat in a skillet. Cook patties, pressing lightly with a spatula in the hot butter, 3 to 5 minutes on each side until browned.

Portobello Bruschetta Mushroom Burger

SERVINGS: 2

Ingredients

1. 8 Roma (plum) tomatoes, diced
2. 1/3 cup chopped fresh basil
3. ¼ cup shredded Parmesan cheese
4. 1 tablespoon balsamic vinegar
5. 2 cloves garlic, minced
6. 1 teaspoon olive oil
7. ½ teaspoon kosher salt
8. ½ teaspoon ground black pepper
9. 2 large Portobello mushroom caps, stems removed
10. 2 tablespoons shredded horseradish Cheddar cheese, or to taste (optional)
11. 2 Kaiser rolls, split

Instructions

1. In a bowl, combine the Roma tomatoes, basil, Parmesan cheese, balsamic vinegar, garlic, olive oil,

kosher salt, and black pepper. Refrigerate for 1 to 2 hours to marinate.
2. Preheat grill for medium heat and lightly oil the grate.
3. Grill Portobello mushrooms with gill sides up on an upper rack of the grill for about 15 minutes, or until hot and juicy. Spoon tomato mix into mushrooms and cover the entire cap. Continue grilling for another 15 to 20 minutes or until heated through.
4. Top with Cheddar cheese if desired, and grill until cheese has melted; about 1 to 2 minutes.
5. Serve on Kaiser Rolls.

Tex-Mex Vegan Burger

SERVINGS: **6**

Ingredients

1. 1/3 cup of white long-grain rice
2. 2 (15-ounce) cans of black beans, rinsed
3. 1 medium shallot, chopped
4. 6 slices of pickled jalapeño
5. 1 tablespoon of barbecue sauce
6. 1 teaspoon of chili powder
7. ½ teaspoon of ground cumin
8. 1 egg white
9. Salt
10. Black pepper
11. 4 tablespoons of vegetable oil, divided
12. 6 hamburger buns
13. Desired condiments

Instructions

1. Cook rice according to package directions. Let cool.
2. Set aside 1/2 cup of beans. Pulse shallot, jalapeño, barbecue sauce, chili powder, cumin, and the rest of the beans in a blender or food processor until a chunky paste forms.
3. Transfer mix to a medium bowl and combine with egg white, rice, and reserved beans. Season with salt and pepper. Form into 6 equal patties. Cover and chill for 1 hour.
4. In a large skillet, heat 2 tablespoons of oil over medium heat. Working in batches of two patties and adding the rest of the oil in between batches, cook until done.
5. Serve with desired condiments on buns.

Spicy Black Bean Burger

SERVINGS: 4

Ingredients

1. 1 (16-ounce) can of black beans, drained, rinsed
2. ½ green bell pepper, cut into slices
3. ½ onion, cut into wedges
4. 3 cloves of garlic, peeled
5. 1 egg
6. 1 tablespoon of chili powder
7. 1 tablespoon of cumin
8. 1 teaspoon of hot sauce
9. ½ cup of bread crumbs

Instructions

1. Preheat oven to 375 degrees F (190 degrees C).
2. Mash black beans into a paste in a medium bowl.
3. In a food processor or blender, chop bell pepper, onion, and garlic, then stir into mashed beans.
4. Combine egg, chili powder, cumin, and hot sauce in a small bowl.
5. Stir egg mix into mashed beans. Mix in bread crumbs. Divide and form into 4 patties.
6. Lightly oil a baking sheet. Place patties on a baking sheet and bake for 10 minutes on each side.
7. Serve.

Garbanzo Bean Burgers

SERVINGS: 4

Ingredients

1. 1 (15 ounce) can garbanzo beans (chickpeas), rinsed and drained
2. 1 red bell pepper, finely chopped
3. 1 carrot, grated
4. 3 cloves garlic, minced
5. 1 red chile pepper, seeded and minced
6. 2 tablespoons chopped fresh cilantro
7. 1 tablespoon tahini paste
8. salt and black pepper, to taste
9. 1 teaspoon olive oil (optional)

Instructions

1. Place garbanzo beans (chickpeas) in a blender or food processor with bell pepper, carrot, garlic, red chile pepper, cilantro, tahini, salt, and pepper. Cover and pulse 5 times. Scrape the sides and pulse until mixed. If the mix is dry, add olive oil. Refrigerate for 30 minutes.
2. Preheat oven to 350 degrees F (175 degrees C).
3. Prepare a baking sheet with parchment paper or lightly grease with cooking spray. Shape the garbanzo bean burger mix into patties.
4. Bake 20 minutes. Flip and bake for 10 minutes more or until evenly browned.

Monterey Jack Eggplant Burgers

SERVINGS: 6

Ingredients

1. 1 eggplant, peeled and sliced into 3/4 inch rounds
2. 1 tablespoon margarine
3. 6 slices Monterey Jack cheese
4. 6 hamburger buns, split
5. 6 leaves lettuce
6. 6 slices tomato
7. ½ onion, sliced
8. ½ cup dill pickle slices
9. 1 (20 ounces) bottle ketchup
10. 3 tablespoons mayonnaise
11. 2 tablespoons prepared yellow mustard

Instructions

1. Place eggplant slices on a microwaveable plate. Cook in microwave for about 5 minutes, or until the center is cooked.
2. In a large skillet, melt margarine over medium-high heat.
3. Fry eggplant slices until toasted lightly on each side. Place a slice of cheese on each slice and cook until cheese has melted.
4. Remove from skillet and place eggplant on hamburger buns. Top with lettuce, tomato, onion, and pickles, and dress with ketchup, mayonnaise and mustard; or any other desired toppings.

Portobello Burgers with Goat Cheese

SERVINGS: 4

Ingredients

1. 2 medium beets
2. ¼ cup olive oil
3. 2 tablespoons balsamic vinegar
4. 1 teaspoon dried rosemary
5. 2 cloves garlic, minced and divided
6. 4 Portobello mushroom caps
7. ½ cup goat cheese
8. 4 sandwich buns, split and toasted
9. 1½ cups baby spinach leaves
10. 3 tablespoons mayonnaise
11. 2 cloves garlic, minced
12. 2 limes, juiced

Instructions

1. Preheat oven to 400 degrees F (200 degrees C).
2. Cut tops off the beets and place them in a dish with enough water to cover the bottom. Roast in the preheated oven for about 40 to 50 minutes, or until you can easily pierce them with a knife. Remove and refrigerate until cool. Slice and set aside.
3. Preheat oven's broiler and set rack to the second level from the heat source.
4. In a bowl, whisk olive oil, balsamic vinegar, rosemary, and 2 cloves minced garlic together. Spread half of this mix over the ribbed side of the Portobello mushroom caps. Arrange mushrooms on a baking sheet with the ribbed sides facing upwards. Broil the mushrooms 5 to 7 minutes or until tender, avoid burning the garlic.
5. Flip mushrooms and brush the remaining olive oil mixture over the tops of the caps. Return to the oven and broil until tender, about 5 minutes. Spread equal amounts of the goat cheese on one half of each of the sandwich rolls. Top each with sliced beets and spinach.
6. Whisk mayonnaise, garlic, and lime juice together in a bowl. Spread evenly over the remaining halves of sandwich rolls and top with one mushroom cap. Bring the two halves together and serve.

Barley Black Bean Burgers

SERVINGS: **4**

Ingredients

1. ½ cup quick-cooking barley
2. 1 cup water
3. 1 (16 ounce) can black beans, drained and rinsed
4. 1 cup shredded Cheddar cheese
5. 1 cup mushrooms, minced
6. ½ onion, minced
7. ½ red bell pepper, minced
8. ¼ cup fresh parsley, minced
9. 2 large eggs
10. 3 cloves garlic, minced
11. salt and ground black pepper, to taste
12. ½ cup bread crumbs, or as needed

Instructions

1. Preheat outdoor grill on high heat and lightly oil the grate. Grease a sheet of aluminum foil with oil.
2. In a saucepan, bring barley and water to a boil. Cover, reduce heat to low, and simmer for 10 to 15 minutes or until the barley is tender.
3. In a large bowl, mash black beans with a fork until thick. Stir barley, Cheddar cheese, mushrooms, onion, red bell pepper, parsley, eggs, garlic, salt, and black pepper into mashed black beans.
4. Mix bread crumbs into bean mixture until a sticky batter forms that holds together. Divide batter into 4 to 6 patties and place on prepared aluminum foil.
5. Grill patties on the aluminum foil for about 8 minutes on each side.

Portobello Mushroom Burger

SERVINGS: **4**

Ingredients

1. 2 tablespoons of olive oil
2. 2 tablespoons of balsamic vinegar
3. 1 tablespoon of Dijon mustard
4. 2 cloves of garlic, minced
5. ½ teaspoon of Worcestershire sauce, optional
6. 1 pinch of salt and pepper
7. 4 large Portobello mushrooms, stems removed
8. 4 hamburger buns

Instructions

1. Preheat grill on medium-high heat. Lightly oil the grate.
2. In a bowl, whisk together olive oil, balsamic vinegar, Dijon mustard, garlic, Worcestershire sauce, salt, and pepper. Brush over tops and bottoms of the mushrooms. Let stand for 10 minutes.
3. Grill mushrooms in covered grill, until browned and tender on both sides.
4. Serve on hamburger buns.

Black Bean Chili Burgers

Ingredients

1. 1 (16 ounce) can black beans, drained and rinsed
2. ½ green bell pepper, cut into 2 inch pieces
3. ½ onion, cut into wedges
4. 3 cloves garlic, peeled
5. 1 egg
6. 1 tablespoon chili powder
7. 1 tablespoon cumin
8. 1 teaspoon Thai chili sauce or hot sauce
9. 1/2 cup bread crumbs

Instructions

1. If you are grilling, preheat outdoor grill for high heat, and oil a sheet of aluminum foil lightly. If baking, preheat oven to 375 degrees F (190 degrees C), and lightly oil a baking sheet.
2. Mash black beans with a fork in a medium bowl until thick and pasty.
3. In a blender or food processor, finely chop bell pepper, onion, and garlic. Combine this mix with the mashed beans.
4. In a small bowl, stir egg, chili powder, cumin, and chili sauce. Stir this mix into mashed beans.
5. Mix in bread crumbs until the mix is sticky. Divide and shape into four patties.
6. If grilling, place patties on foil, and grill for about 8 minutes on each side. If baking, place patties on baking sheet, and bake about 10 minutes on each side.

Tex-Mex Veggie Burger

Ingredients

1. 1/3 cup of white long-grain rice
2. 2 (15-ounce) cans of black beans, rinsed
3. 1 medium shallot, chopped
4. 6 slices of pickled jalapeño
5. 1 tablespoon of barbecue sauce
6. 1 teaspoon of chili powder
7. ½ teaspoon of ground cumin
8. 1 egg white
9. Salt
10. Black pepper
11. 4 tablespoons of vegetable oil, divided
12. 6 hamburger buns
13. Desired condiments

Instructions

1. Cook rice according to package directions. Let cool.
2. Set aside ½ cup beans. Blend shallot, jalapeño, barbecue sauce, chili powder, cumin, and remaining beans by pulsing in a food processor until a chunky purée forms.
3. Transfer purée to a medium bowl and mix in egg white, rice, and reserved beans. Season with salt and pepper. Form into 6 patties, cover, and chill for 1 hour.
4. Heat 2 tablespoons of oil in a large skillet over medium heat. Working in 2 batches and adding the remaining 2 tablespoons oil between batches, cook patties until desired doneness.
5. Serve on buns with desired condiments.

Jamaican Bean Burgers

SERVINGS: **6**

Ingredients

- 2 tablespoons olive oil
- 2 ¼ cups chopped onion
- 3 cloves garlic, minced
- 1 habanero pepper, chopped
- 1 ½ tablespoons grated fresh ginger root
- 1 teaspoon salt
- ¾ teaspoon ground allspice
- ¾ teaspoon ground nutmeg
- 2 ¼ cups cooked black beans, rinsed and drained
- 2 ¼ cups cooked long-grain white rice
- 2 ½ cups dry bread crumbs
- 6 hamburger buns, split

Instructions

1. In a large skillet, heat 1 tablespoon of olive oil over medium heat. Add onions and garlic. Cook and stir for a few minutes. Mix in habanero pepper and cook until tender. Remove from heat and transfer to a bowl.
2. Pour in the beans, rice and bread crumbs. Season with ginger, salt, allspice and nutmeg. Mix well with your hands and form into 6 patties.
3. Heat remaining oil in a large skillet over medium-high heat. Fry the patties for about 10 minutes, or until golden on each side.
4. Serve on buns with your favorite toppings.
1. r side.

Lentil Burgers

SERVINGS: **8**

Ingredients

1. 1 cup dry brown lentils
2. 2 ½ cups water
3. ¼ cup milk
4. 1 cup wheat and barley nugget cereal
5. 1 (1 ounce) envelope dry onion soup mix
6. ½ teaspoon poultry seasoning
7. 2 eggs, beaten
8. ½ cup chopped walnuts
9. 1 cup seasoned dry bread crumbs
10. 2 tablespoons vegetable oil

Instructions

1. In a saucepan, combine lentils and water; and bring to a boil. Cover, reduce heat to low, and simmer until tender, about 30 minutes. Drain the water.
2. Combine the cooked lentils, milk, wheat and barley cereal, eggs and walnuts in a large bowl.
3. Season with onion soup mix and poultry seasoning. Mix well with your hands and let stand for 30 minutes, or refrigerate overnight. Heat oil over medium heat in a large skillet.
4. With an ice cream scoop, scoop out balls of the lentil mix. Drop scoops into bread crumbs, and coat while shaping into patties. Fry in the hot skillet until browned on both sides, about 10 minutes total, depending on patty thickness.

Zucchini Patties

Ingredients

- 2 cups grated zucchini
- 2 eggs, beaten
- ¼ cup chopped onion
- ½ cup all-purpose flour
- ½ cup grated Parmesan cheese
- ½ cup shredded mozzarella cheese
- Salt, to taste
- 2 tablespoons vegetable oil

Instructions

1. Combine zucchini, eggs, onion, flour, Parmesan cheese, mozzarella cheese, and salt in a medium bowl. Stir to distribute ingredients evenly.
2. Heat some oil in a skillet over medium-high heat.
3. Drop zucchini mixture by large tablespoonfuls, cooking for a few minutes on each side until it is golden.

Tofu Burgers

Ingredients

- 1 (12 ounce) package firm tofu
- 2 teaspoons vegetable oil
- 1 small onion, chopped
- 1 celery, chopped
- 1 egg, beaten
- ¼ cup shredded Cheddar cheese
- salt and pepper to taste
- ½ cup vegetable oil, for frying

Instructions

1. In a small skillet, heat 2 teaspoons of vegetable oil.
2. Sauté the onion and celery until lightly browned and soft. Place in a medium bowl and set aside.
3. Squeeze out excess water from tofu. Chop finely and place in bowl with onion and celery. Combine with egg, cheese, salt and pepper until. Heat a large skillet over medium-high heat and pour in 1/2 cup vegetable oil, or enough to be 1/4 inch deep.
4. Drop tofu mixture into pan in 6 equal parts. Flatten to form patties. Fry for 5 to 7 minutes on each side, until golden.

Chickpea Falafel Burgers

Ingredients

1. 1 tablespoon vegetable oil
2. 2 green onions, chopped
3. ¾ cup diced fresh mushrooms
4. 3 cloves garlic, chopped
5. 1 (15.5 ounce) can garbanzo beans, with liquid
6. 1 ½ tablespoons chopped fresh cilantro
7. 1 ½ teaspoons minced fresh parsley
8. 1 ½ tablespoons curry powder
9. ½ teaspoon ground cumin
10. ½ cup dry bread crumbs
11. 2 egg whites
12. 2 tablespoons vegetable oil, or as needed

Instructions

1. In a large skillet, heat 1 tablespoon of oil over medium-high heat. Add green onions and mushrooms. Cook until tender, frequently stirring.
2. In a blender or food processor, combine the garbanzo beans (along with the liquid) and garlic. Blend until smooth. Transfer to a medium bowl and stir in the mushrooms and onions.
3. Mix in cilantro, parsley, curry powder and cumin. Add bread crumbs and egg whites, mixing until well blended.
4. Over medium heat in a large skillet, heat enough oil to cover the bottom. Form bean mix into 4 balls, and flatten into patties. Fry each for about 5 minutes until browned on each side.

Brown Rice Burgers

SERVINGS: 12

Ingredients

1. 2 cups cooked brown rice
2. ½ cup parsley, chopped
3. 1 cup carrot, finely grated
4. ½ cup onion, finely chopped
5. 1 clove garlic, minced
6. 1 teaspoon salt
7. ¼ teaspoon ground black pepper
8. 2 eggs, beaten
9. ½ cup whole wheat flour
10. 2 tablespoons vegetable oil for cooking

Instructions

1. In a medium mixing bowl, combine all ingredients except oil. Form mix into 12 patties, firmly pressing with hands.
2. Add vegetable oil to a skillet and heat over medium heat. Cook patties until brown, about 4-5 minutes per side, turning once.

THANK YOU

Thank you for choosing *Delicious American Burgers on The Grill* for improving your cooking skills! I hope you enjoyed the recipes while making them and tasting them! If you're interested in learning new recipes and new meals to cook, go and check out the other books of the series.

CPSIA information can be obtained
at www.ICGtesting.com
Printed in the USA
BVHW041245030521
606340BV00009B/2385